Poetry to God

Volume 4

PRISON PRAISE
CRY'S FROM BEHIND THE WALL

TERRY WEBB

Order this book online at www.trafford.com
or email orders@trafford.com

Most Trafford titles are also available at major online book retailers.

© Copyright 2014 Terry Webb.

All rights reserved. No part of this publication may be reproduced, stored in a retrieval system, or transmitted, in any form or by any means, electronic, mechanical, photocopying, recording, or otherwise, without the written prior permission of the author.

Printed in the United States of America.

ISBN: 978-1-4907-4221-2 (sc)
ISBN: 978-1-4907-4222-9 (hc)
ISBN: 978-1-4907-4223-6 (e)

Library of Congress Control Number: pending

Because of the dynamic nature of the Internet, any web addresses or links contained in this book may have changed since publication and may no longer be valid. The views expressed in this work are solely those of the author and do not necessarily reflect the views of the publisher, and the publisher hereby disclaims any responsibility for them.

Any people depicted in stock imagery provided by Thinkstock are models, and such images are being used for illustrative purposes only.
Certain stock imagery © Thinkstock.

Trafford rev. 07/25/2014

www.trafford.com
North America & international
toll-free: 1 888 232 4444 (USA & Canada)
fax: 812 355 4082

To my father God

Father God, I truly thank you for keeping me focused and giving
Me strength to follow my dreams as a poet/ writer.
I thank you for your spirit and character showing me the way.
I am forever grateful.

I am grateful for my imagination. I will be open to having
Faith in all possibilities.

I am forever grateful being a part of your creation and being chosen
To write your book **"POETRY TO GOD *Volume 4*"**

SPECIAL DEDICATION

To my father God for protecting and keeping me focused while doing my time in prison. I also want to thank the Lord for giving me both financial and mental support to write and publish this book. I truly love you Lord, and I thank you for everything you have done for me, doing for me and for what you're about to do for me because I know that your mighty hand is upon me...

Foreword

Poetry To God Volume 4 Prison Praise is a vast collection of spiritual, uplifting and Empowering Poems written by a man doing time in State Prison. This book of poetry Includes cries from Behind the wall and love letters from prison. Each poem will Encourage your heart, soul and mind and keep you focused on the things of God. Overwhelming comfort can also be found here in this book of inspirational poetry. All of the poems are true life experiences written by Terry Webb while doing time In a California State Prison keeping his heart and mind on the things of God…

"OUTCASTS"

Locked away, from the civilized race,
We are confined, in this inhumane place.
This life was not, a part of God's plan,
This life was devised by, the plans of man.
God gave man life, He gave it abundantly,
Jails nor prisons were not meant to be.
How can sinful man judge, another sinful man?
When his ways are the same, I don't understand.
No one is perfect, white, brown or black,
When you point your finger, remember three points back!
We are programmed in this system, to hate one another,
Remember the laws of God, He said love thy brother.
But we throw all love, high upon the shelves,
We fight and we kill, destroying ourselves.
Where is brotherly love, where is it, my brother?
Where is the respect, we should have for each other?
We all are locked away, and no longer are we free,
We are all Outcasts, to this Society!

By Terry Webb

"ANOTHER LONELY DAY"

Another lonely day I spend-
Inside this horrid place,
As an outcast to Society-
Far from the civilized race.
I try to hide my pain inside
All sorrow within me,
As I think about the life I had
A life that once was free.
Day's, months, and years pass by
As I sit inside this cell,
I am lost, to the outside world
Confined to living hell.
I am a stranger to this land
My home is far away,
I'm longing, for my place called home
Where my children run and play.
My heart and mind on life is stayed
The visions that I see,
Beyond these prison walls I see
The day that I'm set free.
So I keep my mind upon that thought
No longer in dismay,
But all my thoughts are just a dream
And another lonely day.

By Terry Webb

"FAINT TEARFUL PRAYER"

Although my eyes, are filled with tears,
I have no doubts, or even fears.
Though the mist of sin that shall arise,
And hide the Heavens, starry skies.
The Lord my God, He hears my cry;
High up in heaven, above the sky.
He looks down upon, my tearful face,
And gently apply His loving grace.
He gives His touch, of loving care,
He answers my faint and tearful prayer.

By Terry Webb

"INNER CRY"

To you my Lord I lift up my soul
To you I surrender all,
Upon your love and from your grace
Please break this fatal fall.

Only you, the mighty One
Above the Heavens sky,
You alone, "O" Lord, my God
Can hear my inner cry.

By Terry Webb

"I HAVE SINNED"

By not confessing sin, is a bad thing to do,
It's poison in your system, stand between God and you.
It's easy to say "Lord please forgive me, I have sinned,
He is just to forgive you, that sin is put to end

To man it's very difficult, to come right out and say,
Lord I have sinned, throughout my journey way.
Unlike the prodigal son, he was able to admit fault,
He should have been punished, his other brother thought.

But his loving father forgave him, and blotted out his sin,
He was happy to see his son, and took him back in.
Repenting of your sins, is like rising from the dead,
The father gave the child, a whole new life ahead.

By: Terry Webb

"SILENCE OF MY CELL"

In the silence of my cell
I with my Savior share,
I share my worries, and my troubles
For He alone does care.
He fills my heart with peace and love
He comforts me with grace,
Against the troubles of this world
Within this horrid place.

By: Terry Webb

"CAGE"

Cages were not, intended for man,
They were not, a part of God's plan.
But evil became, a part of man's life,
Now man must live, in bitter strife.

Locked inside, a world of sin,
In cages built, by the hands of men.
But God did not, intend this to be,
When God made man, He made him free!

By Terry Webb

"LAND OF THE LOST"

A place in which the world forgot-
Where criminals do their time,
This place is where you're locked away,
As a consequence to crime.

You're locked behind tall prison walls-
In there you pay the cost,
Regretful pain shall pierce your soul-
In the land of the lost.

In the land of the lost, my friend-
They send you there alone;
Your life will look so strangely dim-
Your future is unknown.

Darkness shall surround your heart-
You'll find no room for love,
Your soul will cry out to the Lord-
And search the sky's above.

"What happened?" is your biggest question;
"My Freedom," where did it go?
Well time is all you'll do now friend,
"You lost," and this I know.

Your life is now a darkened maze-
You now must pay the cost!
You'll do your time, each day of it-
In the Land of the Lost!

By Terry Webb

"GUILT FREE"

All the burdens of my guilt
Is nailed upon the cross
Christ purged my sin in His own blood
No longer am I lost

Through Him my conscience is set free
My sins are cast away
The burdens of my guilt are gone
When Christ died that day

By Terry Webb

"CHANGE ME LORD"

I pray dear Lord, please change my life
That I be more like Thee,
Please change my life to be like yours
That I, a light may be.

See if there is some sin in me
Then cleanse my heart, I pray,
Please help me keep my eyes on Thee
Thy words also obey,

By Terry Webb

TOMORROW IS NOT PROMISED

Tomorrow is not promised and often a question on hold, but God knows exactly how life will unfold.---Luke 12:22 Then Jesus said to his disciples: "Therefore I tell you, do not worry about your life, what you will eat; or about your body, what you will wear. Philippians 4:6 Do not be anxious about anything, but in every situation, by prayer and petition, with thanksgiving, present your requests to God.-1 Peter 5:7 Cast all your anxiety on him because he cares for you. Matthew 6:25 "Therefore I tell you, do not worry about your life, what you will eat or drink; or about your body, what you will wear. Is not life more than food and the body more than clothes?

"LIVING BLIND"

Life will be a darkened maze
No rest or quiet within,
When trouble blows into your life
That leads you into sin.

Lost, you will not find your way
No longer, will you have light,
You've put aside the Living God
Opposing what is right.

The shadow of death is overhead
Your soul is now in fear,
In fear your soul is now, because
Death is ever near.

Blind, you cannot see the path
Of life God has for you,
You're living in a darkened maze
By all the wrong you do.

Now is the time to change your life
And leave the past behind,
You cannot live a peaceful life
By living in the blind.

By Terry Webb

"SHARE MY SORROW"

Comfort me my Lord, I pray-
Heal this heart of mine,
I put my trust in you alone-
Your love it is divine.

The only thing that I have to give-
Is brokenness and strife,
But please, except me as I am-
And beautify my life.

All that I ever had in life-
Is lost or gone away,
Restore to me new life, my Lord-
This to you, I pray.

Forever is your word O Lord-
I surrender myself to Thee,
My life is in your hands dear Lord-
Let blessings fall on me.

Lead me to the living waters-
And be there by my side,
You know my soul is thirsty Lord-
Don't let me be denied.

You told me Lord that you'll be there-
For all of my tomorrow,
O Lord I pray that you would come
And share with me my sorrow.

By: Terry Webb

"MIRROR OF MY LIFE"

It took much grace, to judge myself
My vanity was strong
I could not see the faults I made
Nor admit that I was wrong

Yes, money was my highest goal
My desire was to gain
But drugs enslaved my mind and soul
This caused my life much pain

I hurt the ones whom loved me most
From me, they turned their face
For in their hearts they deeply know
That death was my embrace

But at my lowest point in life
I turned to God whom knew
Just how to turn my life around
And show what I must do

He showed me how to live my life
To show no disrespect
He said I am to live for Him
Christ's life I should reflect

He said to keep in mind my past
The life I led in sin
Then guard well each step I take
Lest I go back again

He said to keep in mind my past
The heartache and the strife
And keep in mind the mirror
The Mirror of My Life

By: Terry Webb

"JUST LIKE YOU"

There is a little boy at home
Watching night and day,
For the day that you'll come back
To be with him always.
His little hands are eager to
Do everything yours do,
Yes, that little boy is dreaming
To someday be like you.
This wide eyed little fellow
Believes you're always right,
No one can tell him differently
You're precious in his sight.
In this little fellows mind
No suspicions ever rise,
You're that little fellow's idol
The wisest of the wise.
His wide eyes are upon you
He'll do just what you do,
Remember that this little fellow
Wants to be like you!

By: Terry Webb

"1 MORE DAY"

One more day that passes me by,
I lift my head up towards the sky.
To thank the Lord for helping me,
And reminding me I'll soon be free.
So on my knees to God I pray,
Thanking him for one more day.

By Terry Webb

"ONE MORE DAY"

You have a chance to change your life-
And live a life that's free,
So think about the wrongs you've done-
That brought you here with me.

Behind these prison walls, my friend-
This life should not be you,
You need to really think about
Your life that was not true.

How can you ever win in life?
When will you ever change?
In here you are behind these walls-
And you think it kind of strange.

You need to stop and check yourself-
Do you like being without?
Do you think your woman is waiting on you?
Being a perfect girl scout?

So think about your life, my friend;
There is a better way,
You cannot live each month or year-
Counting one more day!

By: Terry Webb

WHEN WE HURT THE PERSON WE LOVE

When we hurt a person we love, we often wish we hadn't done it. We mourn or feel awful about what we did. Then we say we're sorry and ask that person's forgiveness. When the person forgives us, it is like he or she is "erasing" our mean action. Just like we sometimes hurt the people we love, we also hurt God when we sin. But when we confess our sins to God, He forgives us through Jesus (1st John 1:9 If we confess our sins, he is faithful and just and will forgive us our sins and purify us from all unrighteousness. Hebrews 8:12 12 For I will forgive their wickedness and will remember their sins no more." Let us Pray: Father God, Please help us remember to seek your forgiveness whenever we sin. And please help us to forgive others when they sin against us also, In Jesus name we pray, Amen…

"GOOD-BYE COCAINE"

Dear cocaine, this letter I'm writing
To you is to say good-bye
You only caused me torment and pain
And hurt that made me cry
My heart I gave to you, Cocaine
I really loved you too
Cocaine you were the world to me
I would have died for you
Everything that was valuable to me
My car, my clothes, my gold
Even my household appliances
For you, cocaine I sold
You made me steal from everyone
Even my sisters and my brother
But the lowest thing you made me do
Was stealing from my own mother
You made me beg and borrow for you
And I knew that I was wrong
But you had me hooked on you cocaine
My desire for you was strong
I could not see that I was lost
Blind I could not see
How could I have been too blind to see?

That you were using me
You brought me down to my lowest point
You took my self-esteem
Because of you I went to prison
I wished it was all a dream
But no, with you it was not a dream
Your lusts I did obey
You took my mind and then my heart
You lead me damnations way
Cocaine you were my greatest pain
You used me and abused me
I'm tired of risking my life for you
I want to be set free
It's time to say good-bye to you
You've only caused me pain
The life I spent with you cocaine
There was no life to gain
But now I've found a better friend
The Lord Jesus whom reins on high
Cocaine it's time that we separate
It's time we say Good-Bye!

By: Terry Webb

"MARRIED TO COCAINE"

So now my friend, you've grown tired to grass,
L.S.D., angel dust, pills and even hash.
Now someone pretending to be your friend,
Introduced you to something worse than heroin.
This friend introduced you, to miss cocaine,
A powerful deadly drug, that drives you insane.
But before you start fooling with that glass Jeanie,
Let me just inform you, of how it will be.
The Jeanie will seduce you, and make you her slave,
Stronger men than you, she has sent to their grave.
And to think you would never, become a disgrace,
To end up addicted, to cocaine's sweet taste.
You started out puffing, one afternoon,
Now you will puff away life, soon and very soon.
You will need lots of money, as you have been told,
Because cocaine my friend, is more expensive than gold.

You'll swindle your mother, and just for a buck,
You will turn into something, vile and corrupt.
You'll steal, lie and rob, for one more hit,
You'll feel contentment, and not want to quit.
And the day when you realize, the monster you've grown,
You'll solemnly swear, to leave miss cocaine alone.
But it's hard to shake this drug, to get her off your back,
You will only crave for more, and that's a proven fact.
That glass Jeanie will make you do more,
Sending you right back, to the dope man's door.
You desperately get more from the pusher, and then,
You welcome miss cocaine, in your heart again.
You'll want more and more, just as she foretold,
Giving miss cocaine, your mind body and soul.
You'll give up your morals, your conscience and heart,
Married to cocaine, "UNTIL DEATH DO YOU PART."

"FROM OLD TO NEW"

There was a certain man on drugs,
All things he did was sin,
He did not care of the things he did,
Or the wrong he did to men.
This man was so corrupt he was,
In every given way,
Seems this man just could not change
The life he lived each day.

Then someone told this man one day,
That he was going to hell,
He pushed aside the things they said,
Till prison became his jail.
Then something burned inside him,
What he heard was not a lie,
He knew that he was lost in sin,
If suddenly he should die.

Time went on and on and on,
Memories haunting him inside,
Until this man could take no more,
Then he prayed until he cried.
He did what he was told to do,
And he repented all his sin,
JESUS came into his heart
And gave him Life again.

That day a certain change took place,
JESUS regained control,
He reached his hand out to this man,
And pulled him from Satan's hold.
And now this man he lives for God,
In all things he say and do,
The LORD gave a new Life to him,
And can do the same for you.

By: Terry Webb

"CHILDHOOD PAST"

I looked back at my life one day
For just a little while,
I was turning the pages of my past
Till I saw myself a child.

I laughed at all the wondrous things
That I had done before,
But I only sit in memory of this
I'll see these day's no more.

Each page I read of my childhood life
Brought joy unto my heart,
My sisters and brothers had Godly love
Always together, never apart.

There was a special love in our hearts
In everything we did,
Our hearts were so very pure back then
Our love could not be hid.

As a child we never had to worry
About anything in this world,
Because God, He had His arms around us
He loved each boy and girl.

Every Sunday we all went to church
To the palace of our King,
I can remember certain poems I read
Even songs I had to sing.

Life was so very simple back then
Where did my childhood go?
Day's and months, even years went by
Into a man, I had to grow!

By Terry Webb

"GIVING MY HEART"

I give unto you Lord, my one and only heart-
That you will come inside, and never ever part,
Please place pure love inside, cleanse of all defect-
Please except my heart "O" Lord, please do not reject.

My heart is without blemish; my heart can now be true-
This is why "O" Lord my God I give my heart to you,
Please place pure love inside me, let me be an offering-
I give to you my very heart, "It is all I have to bring."

By: TERRY WEBB

"ANOTHER DAY"

You brought me through, another day,
My heart is glad, to you it pray.
I give you praise, cause you let me see,
Another day, of life for me.

By Terry Webb

"COMING HOME"

I'm tired of sin and straying away
"O" Lord, I'm coming home,
I'll trust in Thee and trust Thy love
Never no more I'll roam.

My heart is warm toward Thee, "O" Lord
I feel real good this way,
I will remain just as I am
Never again to stray.

By: Terry Webb

"GOD IS TO ME"

God is my refuge, He is my shield,
He fights my battles, on the battle field.
When I cry for help, my God is there,
For those He loves, because He cares.

For me God is, my guiding light,
His Word to me is pure delight.
"For me," I'm just a mortal man;
But, I rest in God's, unchanging hand.

By Terry Webb

"LOST AND FOUND"

Lost and confused, in a world of sin,
With a broken heart, that needs a mend.
Going here and there, and yet don't know,
Where you should be or where you should go.
Until at last, you began to pray,
Something changed, in your life that day.
You began to see, a brand new life,
Instead of the old, with bitter strife.
You found peace, inside the Lord,
He became your shield and sword.
Nothing in life, could not compare,
With the love you found, within the Lord's care.
You're no longer lost, and not confused,
Within this world, being abused.
For the Lord has brought, you out of strife,
He gave to you, a better life.
A life of love, and tender care,
With the Lord Jesus, always there.

By Terry Webb

PSALM 102:17

"He will respond to the prayer of the destitute; He will not despise their plea." ----Being destitute means that we are missing what is essential (food, water, clothes, hope, etc) and not being able to acquire it our self. You probably have a roof over your head, food, water, and even clothes to put on your body. But, however, you may be trapped in sin with a bad habit, you may feel alone, overlooked and underappreciated, living an empty dream, overwhelmed by stress, or hurting beyond words. There are many ways to arrive at an experience of being destitute. One blessing that everyone shares is the ability to call out to God in any and every situation. In this psalm, an afflicted man is pouring out his soul to God. There is comfort in knowing that God does not despise your plea. In fact, our prayers out of sincere desperation, disappointment, and pain touch God's heart. God will rebuild lives and shine His glory where there are only ruins.

"HERE I AM"

Here I am "O" Lord, my God
My life I give to Thee,
To let Thy works be done through me
God willing let it be.
Unwavering faith that never doubts
The good you choose to do,
Here I am "O" Lord, my God
My life, I give to you.

By Terry Webb

"LIFE OF SORROW"

Another day of loneliness, still at my side,
I want to be free from this hell, Oh how I've tried.
One more day of my life, has come to an end,
My heart is broken into pieces, and it will not mend.

Tell me how much longer Lord, will it be this way,
Will it be always and forever, or just another day.
Tell me how much longer Lord, will prison be my life,
Will I forever go through sorrow, and the bitter strife?

Seems the world I live in Lord, nobody seems to care,
Animosity, hate, murder and rape are filled within the air.
But I know one day O Lord my God, you will set me free,
From this life of sorrow and hell, hate and animosity.

By: Terry Webb

"WITH ME STILL"

Each day that come, and passes me by,
I sometimes wonder, I sometimes cry.
Because of pain, deep down inside,
No one knows, because it I hide.
Day after day, when I open each eye,
I try to make things better, oh how I try.
My heart is filled, with nothing but gloom,
Each day and moment, I'm locked in this room.
I wonder why can't, I live life free,
Why can't people, just let me be.
My life seems to be, just passing me by,
As I look at the clouds, up in the sky.
Seems I'm lost, what can I do?
My heart talked to me, and gave me a clue.
Reminding me of Jesus, how much He care,
Telling me His presence is always there.
My heart said "Jesus," will always fulfill,
I'm glad to know, He's with me still.

By Terry Webb

"CHANGE MY LIFE"

"O" Lord, My God, rejuvenate me
With your love this day.
With your wisdom, also your teachings
Change my life, I pray.
It is above all else I ask
I cry, "O" Lord, please hear,
I am Thy (prodigal son) whom cries
Repentance to Thy ear.

By Terry Webb

"THE INCREDIBLE ONE"

God is good and He is great
So every morning you awake
You should say "Thank you Father" for another day
It's not hard to do or say
Just give Him the praise that He wants us to
That's all he really wants us to do
You know it's rewarding, and precious and fun,
Knowing you're a child of the "Incredible One."

By: Terry Webb

"I AM HIS"

I am the Lord's, and the Lord is mine,
His Word is truth, and love divine.
I am His, for whatever He choose,
I am His, if He chooses to use.
Here I am, for all eternity,
With my Lord, who set me free.
My life was rough, yes, upon every road,
Until I met God, to help carry my load.
Forever and always, I am with Thee,
Forever and always, I am free.
I am His, for the life He gave me,
I am His, through all eternity.

By Terry Webb

"LIFE GOES ON"

Locked away, inside a cell,
A living nightmare, a living hell.
Locked away, from society,
Where bars and walls, is all you see.

Inside a small, four cornered room,
Where day by day, you sit in gloom.
It's where you eat, and where you sleep,
It's where you think, and where you weep.

Life has stopped for you, you're bound,
While the outside world, turn round and round.
Locked away, you're all alone,
While the outside world, "Life goes on."

By Terry Webb

"WHY WE MUST SUFFER"

Tell me why in this life, we must suffer so,
Please, tell me why, so that I might know.
Sin entered man, from his disobedience,
Forgiveness came from one man's obedience.

Christ Jesus suffered, He endured life's pain,
He took man's sin that we might gain.
A new relationship, with God the creator,
He gave His life, to be our mediator.

For this reason, we must suffer also,
We must suffer, in order to grow.
So pick up thy cross, and follow the Lord,
The spirit of God is your shield and sword.

By Terry Webb

THE RAGING STORM

God is always right there next to you even if the storm is raging and you can't sense His presence. He promised that He would never leave you nor forsake you. The key is to figure out how to get your eyes off of the storm, and on the One who can help you calm it. Do you remember the story in scripture where Jesus came walking on the water? Matt: 14:22-32 the disciples in the boat were terrified of both the storm and this figure they saw coming towards them. We would've been also. However, in the midst of their confusion and fear, Jesus spoke revealing himself and telling them there was no reason to be afraid. We don't know how the others in the boat responded, but Peter; bold, courageous, impetuous, and dangerous Peter; decided he wanted to walk out to Jesus. And, he did…for a while. The storm was raging, but Peter was walking. The water churned beneath Him, but he was so captivated by the One who had given him permission to walk on the water, that he didn't even notice. At first that is. After a while, he got a little confident and decided to look around. That is when the circumstances got the best of him. When he took his eyes off of Jesus, he began to sink. But, Jesus was right there next to him. The Savior of the World picked him up and put him in the boat. So let us keep our eyes off of the storm, and look towards Jesus, the one who can help us calm it.

"CLOSER TO THE LORD"

Get closer to the Lord, as the days go on,
Get under His care, stop lingering on.
God has a purpose, for both you and I,
A purpose for all things, in and under the sky.
Get closer to the Lord, kneel to him and pray,
Win souls for Him, each perilous day.
He will lead you in truth, all your day long,
Each day of your lifetime, be in Him strong!

By Terry Webb

"A STRAIGHT ROAD"

Look over your shoulder, take a look back–
To see that your walk, was strictly off track,
From one side of the road, then on to the other–
Then into a ditch, and later in another.
Walking with the Lord, your path is made straight–
Now on a straight road, towards Heaven's gate,
All cracks are gone; it's a smooth road–
With Jesus now helping, carry up your load.

By: TERRY WEBB

"CHOSEN FOR A PURPOSE"

Chosen for a purpose, yet I do not know-
But I must now follow; go where I must go,
Chosen by the Lord, who called on me so clear-
Gave to me a purpose, to follow up this year.

The Lord He have appeared to me, and unto you-
With a chosen purpose, for all mankind to do,
To lift His Holy name, and pray on bending knee-
That is mankind's purpose, now that we are free.

By: **TERRY WEBB**

"DEVOTION"

"O" Lord my God, my life is you
I live my life, gloriously too
My actions today, I desire to be
Prepared for Your, return to me
So take my life, and use it today
In Jesus name, to you I pray

By: Terry Webb

"FOR YOU MY LORD"

For you my Lord, my heart cannot erase
The beautiful smile you put upon my face
You gave to me a life worthwhile
For you my Lord, I cannot defile
For you have done, so much for me
Out of bondage, you have set me free
For you my Lord, Jesus my King
I give to you, this song I sing

By: Terry Webb

"WHERE MUST I GO?"

"O" Lord my God, what must I do?
To make my life alright with you?
What steps must I chose, what steps do I take?
What path "O" Lord, should I choose to make?
"O" Lord I'm lost, I cannot see,
The path in life, you've chosen for me.
Please tell me Lord, that I might know-
Where in life, You want me to go!

By Terry Webb

"HELLO MY LORD"

Hello my Lord, how are you today,
It's me again, with more words to say.
First of all Lord, on bending knees I pray,
I thank you ever so dearly, for another day.
Thank you for the flowers, and the birds that sing,
You made them all O Lord, each and every thing.
I thank you for keeping my mind, stayed upon you,
I thank you for all things O Lord, all the things you do
But most of all I thank for the new life you've given me,
On the happy road to destiny, with life eternally.

By Terry Webb

"IN DEBT WITH THE LORD"

Always was I in trouble,
But the Lord pulled me through,
He helped me, and He saved me,
When no one wanted too.
He pulled me from Satan's grasp,
On the down count of three,
He pushed him back and told him,
This one belongs to me.
And now I live my life for God,
In each and every way,
I truly thank the Lord above,
For saving me that day.
The Lord is truly wonderful,
His Word, He has kept,
And I will always remember
I'm forever in His debt.

By Terry Webb

"A BETTER WAY"

What is this world coming to?
What is society today?
What can we do to stop all hate?
There has to be some way.

Why do we get involved in drugs?
And gangs to kill each other?
Where is the love God said to have?
He said to love thy brother.

Why must we all destroy ourselves?
With racism and confusion?
Why must our hearts be filed with hate?
There must be some solution.

It hurts me to my heart to see-
Most people's eyes are dim,
They put aside the one true God-
They're unaware of Him.

We need to lift our eyes on high-
To seek the Lord above,
Our hearts we need to give to Him-
That we may have His love.

There has to be a better way-
For society today,
God is the answer for this problem-
He is the better way…

By: TERRY WEBB

"PARDONED"

My life has been a darkened maze-
From God, I had turned,
Although I knew that I was wrong-
His love I had spurned.

A prison cell became my home-
Confined with all my woes,
And no one knew my inner pain-
But God whom always knows.

One day I poured my heart to Him-
Inside that wretched place,
He heard my cry then set me free-
I live now by His grace.

By Terry Webb

"THIS WRETCHED MAN"

Just as I am "O" Lord my God
I beg of Thee receive,
This wretched person that I am
In Thee I do believe.
For Thee, whose blood can cleanse my soul
And rid each sinful spot,
"O" precious Lamb of God, my Lord
Please rid me of each blot.
Search me Lord, and know my heart
I come to Thee this day,
Try me Lord, and know my thoughts
Please hear me as I pray.
Cleanse me of this wretched person
Way down deep inside,
Cleanse me Lord, I pray to Thee
Of sin I try to hide.
This wretched man, I beg of Thee
Please make Him disappear,
For all I need in Thee to find
Thy words teach me to fear.

By Terry Webb

"SINNER'S CRY"

Life's troubles overwhelms my soul
My heart cries out in pain,
O Lord I plead my cause to you
What peace am I to gain?

Forgive me for the wrong I've done
I need you by my side,
I call on your most Holy name
Don't let me be denied.

Today I stand condemned O Lord
Before the law I stand,
Cleanse me of my sinful past
To your perfect demand.

You said that you'll be there for me
No matter what the cost,
I need you more than ever Lord
Right now for I am lost.

You said that if I call your name
And trust in you alone,
Your blood will wash away my past
My sins you will atone.

So I call upon your name "O" Lord
And please don't pass me by,
I beg of Thee, O Lord my God
Please hear this sinners cry!

By: Terry Webb

"THE RAIN"

Sitting in my prison cell, I watch the falling rain,
Beating against the rooftops, and my window pane.
The sky is very dark and the clouds colored gray,
Rain drops falling down, all throughout the day.
The mighty wind is rough, and strong is the breeze,
Blowing the course of rain, breezing through the trees.
I watched the falling rain falling down from the sky,
Sitting in my prison cell, the rain pass me by.

By: Terry Webb

"WIPE MY PAST AWAY"

"O" Lord please help me to forget
The heartache and the tears,
Please "O" Lord wipe away my past
All those painful years.

Help me redeem this present time
To dwell amongst the just,
Give me the protection that I will need
For I've made your name my trust.

Please wipe away my past "O" Lord
And give me a future view,
Please lord wipe away my past
So I may live for you.

By Terry Webb

"LORD, REMEMBER ME"

No room for the meek-
No room for the mild,
Prison is no place-
For an innocent child.
The nights are so lonely-
I toss in my bed,
The days are so dreary-
I face them with dread.
Grant me one prayer-
As you did from the cross,
For that thief who knew-
That his life was a loss.
Please come to this prison-
Where I sit here alone,
Surrounded by wire-
Guard towers and stone.
Broken and penitent-
Forgotten and lost,
On the ash heap of regret-
Where my life was last tossed.
I've no other place-
Left upon this here earth,
Remember me "O" Lord-
Renew me by birth.
Please come to this prison-
And enter my cell,
Save me, "O" Lord-
From the clutched of hell.
If in this life-
My chains are not set free,
In Your Kingdom of Forgiveness-
Lord, Please Remember Me!

By Terry Webb

"I'VE HAD ENOUGH"

"O" Lord my God I pray to thee, please hear me as I cry,
Pain is deep within my heart, and tears are in my eye.
This life has beat me down "O" Lord
and I'm asking you to give,
A new life to me "O" Lord my God that I again may live.

No longer in this life will I continue living this way,
Please "O" Lord I ask of you, hear my prayer today.
I've had enough of this old world, and my awful brutal life,
Nothing but pain, tears of sorrow and hard bitter strife.

I've had enough of this wretched life, all the things around,
Drugs, Prison, institutions and death,
no life for me is found.
Please "O" Lord I ask of you, hear my prayer today.
"O" Lord I'm tired, I've had enough,
I cannot live this way.

By: Terry Webb

"THIS IS IT!"

You get to a point in your life
When you're tired and fed up,
Like a molting volcano
That is about to erupt.
"THIS IS IT!"

You're under so much pressure
Problems beating your brain,
Trying to word them out before
They drive you insane.
"THIS IS IT!"

Trouble everywhere I go, I'm tired of all this worry,
Holding my head down, and always feeling sorry.
<u>This is it</u> - my last time, being arrested by the law,
<u>This is it</u>- my last time behind prison bars in awe.
<u>This is it</u> - the last time, for me being put down,
<u>This is it</u>- no more, being shuffled around.
"THIS IS IT!"

By Terry Webb

"BEING NEAR TO GOD"

I will be near to my Lord, my Lord be near to me,
For He will guide my footsteps, and enable me to see.
I go to His house for worship, His presence I feel so near,
I feel his Spirit inside me; His love is ever so dear.

I truly love the house of God, that's
where His presence dwells,
Where all His people worship Him,
and His Holy Spirit prevail.
I long to always be with Him, in the company of my Lord,
Under his wings and his mercy,
behind His shield and sword!

By: Terry Webb

"FREE"

Prison life was once my life-
Locked away was I,
Trapped behind those prison walls-
My heart in pain did cry.

Time is all I seemed to have-
And prison life was hard,
I stayed within my cell always-
And read about the Lord,

Old Satan had his demons placed-
In that prison all around,
But under the wings of God I was-
There His grace I found.

The love of God became my pillow-
Soft, healing and wide,
So I rested my soul, in His comfort-
In His calm I did abide.

Though prison was a darkened maze-
Ruled by its harsh demands,
I now am free from prison life-
The rules and stern commands.

For God has sent His only Son-
To set all captives free,
Yes, I was bound, but now I'm free-
God proved His love for me.

By Terry Webb

"GIVING THANKS"

I give you thanks "O" Lord, my God
For all you've done for me
To you I give my thanks dear Lord
From sin you set me free

"O" Lord you have been merciful
You heard my inner cry
I give my thanks to you alone
You did not pass me by

By: Terry Webb

"GOD IS ALWAYS THERE"

The Lord is in this place
He is always there,
He is always near you
You're his child and he care.
The Lord is always there my friend
Everywhere you go,
The Lord is omnipotent
And there is nothing he doesn't know.

God will let you know my friend
That his presence is with you,
He will watch and guide you
In all things you say and do.
So remember that the Lord our God
He really truly care,
And everywhere you go my friend,
He is also there.

By: Terry Webb

"BROUGHT BACK"

Although sometimes I stray from you
And disregard Your Word,
In tenderness you bring me back
To be with you O Lord.

Lord tell me why you love me so
Why do you even care?
But mine is not to question why
I'm just glad you're there.

By: Terry Webb

"LEGACY"

Take my hand and show me the way
Let my light so shine,
Please, let me be a blessing to all
Remembered by all mankind.

By letting them see, the life I lived
Was strictly unto Thee,
Shining in beauty, with love for all
As you were unto me.

By Terry Webb

"SO CLOSE TO DEATH"

One day I came so close to death–
    Seemed I could not hide,
I was lost inside its massive shadow–
    There was no hope, I cried.

So close to death that day I came–
    Death had its hold on me,
I knew that there was no way out–
    Then appeared, "Calvary"

I saw the King of Kings my Lord–
    Dying upon the cross,
He said to me: "Your life is spared–
    My life has paid your cost!"

"My blood is shed to give you life,"
    "Come now unto me!"
"In me my child you now must live–
    My grace has set you free."

So close to death, but Christ the Lord–
    He lifted me from harm,
He held my hand within His hand–
    And led me from alarm.

He said that He would be with me–
    Throughout my endless days,
He took me out the hands of death–
    For this I give Him praise!

By Terry Webb

"A NEW HEART"

Create in me a new heart my Lord
Un charmed by this worlds delight,
To things that are higher in you "O" Lord
This world has allured my sight.

I seek the presence of you my God
That you may brighten each day,
Give me a heart to be open to you
So that you may guide my way.

By Terry Webb

"SOMETHING BEAUTIFUL"

Al I had to offer the Lord,
Was brokenness and strife.
But He accepted me as I was,
And He beautified my life.

He made me something beautiful,
He made me something good.
Through all the confusion in my life,
Jesus, He understood.

By Terry Webb

"I WALK WITH THE LORD"

I trod through each day, and as I walk along,
I hum to the Lord, singing to Him a song.
The Lord be right beside me, walking along the way,
He is always by my side, each and every day.
I walk with the Lord, and He walks with me,
He guide and leads the way, enabling me to see.
I trust the Lord and love Him, in every single way,
I walk with Him, talk with Him, each and every day.

By Terry Webb

"A NEW LIFE"

Dear Lord in Heaven, please forgive my sin,
Cleanse me before, my fatal end.
You know that I am, a terrible sinner,
Make me whole, make me a winner.
Please O Lord, the giver of life,
Lift me from, this bitter strife.
O Lord in Heaven, creator of men,
Give me a new life, let this one end

By Terry Webb

"MAKE ME FREE"

Tell me Lord, please let me know,
Why do this life, hurt me so.
What must I do, to live life free?
Please dear Lord, take these chains off me.

By Terry Webb

"GOOD MORNING GOD"

Good morning God, and my Lord,
For awaking me, to be on guard.
Help me fight, in this new day,
To conquer evil, this I pray.
Good morning Lord, and my God,
Help me through, this day I trod.

By Terry Webb

"I'M READY"

Take my life, and let it be
Cleansed of all past sin,
I'm ready to do your service, Lord
Touch me deep within.
Let your love flow deep inside
Your will in me be done,
"O" Heavenly Father, I pray to Thee,
To make me like Your Son!

By Terry Webb

"MY HIDING PLACE"

Even within my prison cell–
Within my darkest hour,
The Lord, He gives me peace of mind–
And bless me with His power.

He lets me know that He is there–
His grace for me abound,
I am His and shall dwell with Him–
In Heaven I shall be found.

By: Terry Webb

"NEVER FROM HIS CARE"

The eyes of the Lord are upon me
He sees everything I do,
The arms of the Lord are around me
I'm safe and I am secure.

Though there were times I knew that I
Had strayed from His will,
The Lord my God He pulled me back
The Lord, he loves me still.

By: Terry Webb

"INSEPARABLE"

The Lord He will not let my soul
Wonder and be lost,
He will not lose me from His hand
No matter what the cost.

For I am bought by such a price
His life He gave for me,
I am held fast within His hand
For all Eternity.

By Terry Webb

"MY HEART MADE TRUE"

Please dear Lord I ask of you
Please live within my heart,
For it is truly broken my Lord
It is torn all apart.
I ask of you to mend this heart
That it may be for you,
And add a touch of love "O" Lord,
So my heart will then be true.

By: Terry Webb

"O HOLY SPIRIT"

"O" Holy Spirit of God please come
Dwell in this heart of mine
Please come and fill my bounty cup
"O" Holy Spirit divine

For I give complete control to you
To cast down every throne
That you may reign supreme in me
And reign supreme alone

By: Terry Webb

"LORD TAKE MY TEARS"

"O" Father in Heaven, who reign on high-
Above the clouds, far beyond the sky,
Hear my plea, please hear my cry;
Take away these tears, from my eyes.
"O" Lord my God, the most high,
Don't overlook, or pass me by.

By Terry Webb

"MAKE ME RIGHT"

Oh Dear Lord, I love you so
I want to do what's right,
I love you and I want to do
What's pleasing to your sight.

Help me to fear sins consequence
Cleanse me from within,
Help me acknowledge when I'm wrong
And be alert to sin.
Please help me in my walk of life
To be pleasing in your sight.
Oh Dear Lord, I love you so
Help me do what's right,

By Terry Webb

"SEIZE THIS TIME"

I ask you to consider
This time you have for rest,
For God directs your steps in life
Give to Him your best.
Yesterday is gone for us
Tomorrow is yet unknown,
Use this time, get close to God
The choice is yours alone.
It matters not what others do
For God is in control,
He sometime places you in a cell
To cleanse and save your soul.
Fight the fight of faith and rest
Surely you'll be blest,
Seize this time and give to God
Your all and all, your best.

By: Terry Webb

"TAKE ME BACK"

Take me back "O" Lord my God
Down on my bending knee's,
For I have strayed away from you
Please take me back, please.
I pray that you would take me back
To where I first received,
"O" Lord I pray you take me back
To when I first believed.
Please let me do the things I did
All things you had me do,
When I was a humble servant of yours
And my heart was open to you.
Just as the prodigal son left home
Then returned to his father one day,
"O" Lord I pray that you take me back
On my bending knee's I pray.

Terry Webb

"USE ME LORD"

"O" Lord my God I humbly ask
For strength to do your will
To you I offer myself right now
Your purpose to fulfill

Use me as you wish, My Lord
Use me as your slave
And may I bring a great reward
When lifted from my grave

By Terry Webb

"SUICIDE"

One evening my heart burned and cried
When a friend of mine talked of suicide
I could have turned my face to hide
But the words of God I had to abide
If I had not just even tried
He may just have committed suicide
I talked to him, giving him self pride
Touching his feelings, deep down inside
He really wanted to live but the coward inside
Was hurting him and stripping him of his self pride
I really feel good now, real good inside
Because I talked him out of committing suicide
But if I had not just even tried
That day my friend, just may have died

By Terry Webb

"POETIC PRAYER"

Dear Lord, Trouble overwhelms our soul
That's why we need you here,
Satan has his demons stirred
"O" Lord we need you near.
We cannot fight this fight alone
We need you by our side,
With you "O" Lord, we know we'll win
Cause our faith in you abide.
Guide us in your way's "O" Lord
Please guide us day by day,
Let your word dwell in our hearts
Lest from thy truth we stray.
Guide and lead us in thy truth
Our Hearts, souls and mind,
Take our hand and lead the way
Be our light, for we are blind.

By Terry Webb

Romans 12:2

"And be not conformed to this world: but be ye transformed by the renewing of your mind, that ye may prove what is that good, and acceptable, and perfect, will of God." So let us all pray: O Lord God whom art in Heaven, Please help us to not be conformed to this world. Let us all be a good example as an ambassador of heaven on earth. Let us all be children of the light O Lord, because you said in your word: 1st John 1:7 If you walk in the light as he is in the light we have fellowship one with another, and the blood of His son Jesus, cleanses us from all sin. Father God, we pray for your blessings to be upon us today in the name of Jesus Christ, with much love and thanksgiving. Amen!.

"SAVE ME LORD"

Hear my cry, "O" Lord, my God
Attend unto my prayer,
From deep within my prison cell
I cry unto you there.
Deliver me from the evil one
Also from bloody men,
I plead your precious blood right now
Lord, save me from my sin.
Save me, Lord, I pray to thee
Gracious God, Almighty King,
Please help me face another day
That I, in you may sing.
Out of my prison cell I cry
To Thee, "O" Lord, my God,
Please take my hand and guide my step
On every road I trod!

By: Terry Webb

"FOREVER YOURS"

I'm forever yours, you're forever mine,
Only you my Lord, you are divine.
For you have showed your love to me
Only you, my Lord, have set me free.

One day I cried to you in pain,
When I cried, it was not in vain.
Forever yours, I am to Thee,
Because you my Lord, first loved me.

By Terry Webb

"GOD LIFTED ME"

Thank you O Lord, for this new day,
Give heed to my voice, for to you I pray.
From the gates of death, you lifted me,
From the hand of Satan, You set me free.

Thy name, my voice, will always prevail,
You have lifted me, from the gates of hell.
I'll always remember, how you brought me through,
I'll praise your name, in all things I do.

By Terry Webb

"SET ME FREE"

Make me free "O" Lord," please set me free
Take away this pain, and suffering from me
Make me whole, "O" Lord," take my strife
Please give to me, a peaceful life

By: Terry Webb

"WHAT HE DONE FOR ME!"

He has delivered me from trouble
When no one else was there,
And even when someone was there
They didn't really care.
He protect me from all evil
Each night and every day,
That's why I devote my life to Him
And to Him I only pray.
He has blest me in so many ways
And has helped in all I do
But most of all He gave His life
For this I love Him too!

By Terry Webb

"BE RIGHTEOUS"

A righteous man, is upright and true-
In all things, he says and do.
A wicked man in all his ways-
Will follow evil all his days.
His life corrupt, his life in sin-
Will follow him until, his life end.
Be righteous, and you will find-
Love, joy, and a peaceful mind.

By Terry Webb

"SET FREE"

Through Christ Jesus, the law of the spirit-
Of life set me free,
From the fatal law of both sin and death-
He has lifted me.
He knows that I can't live for Him
Within my own power,
So he equips me to do, whatever He ask
Each day every hour.
So I thank you Lord for setting me free,
For the grace you've given to me.
I thank you Lord, for your Holy Spirit
And love that lives in me.

By: Terry Webb

"SURRENDER"

Confined behind these prison walls-
Where I am just a stranger,
With no remorse within my soul-
And blind to all my danger.

Discouraged in my situation-
Where I have no control,
I'm locked inside a prison cell-
No light within my soul.

I'm locked away for what I've done-
Yet more and more each day,
I find myself upon my knees-
To God in Christ I pray.

Loneliness overwhelms my soul-
It cuts me like a knife,
Oh Lord, I pray that you would come
To heal and nourish my life.

I pray that you would come by me-
To heal my aching soul,
Also to heal my heart Oh Lord-
My life, Lord take control.

By Terry Webb

"TURNED FROM SIN"

Teach me how to live "O" Lord
And do all things you say,
Please help me be a loving child
One who will obey.
Please wash away my sins "O" Lord
And turn them all to rend,
Make my sins as white as snow
And let me live again.
Please lend your ear to me "O" Lord
Please hear what I must say,
I want to live for you dear Lord
Today and every day.
Give to me another chance
For I know that I can stand,
And only live for you my Lord
I will be a better man.
Guided by Your mighty hand
I'll be just and holy too,
Lifting up your Holy name
I'll bring glory unto you.

By Terry Webb

"LOVE LETTERS FROM PRISON"

"A MEMORY OF YOU"

These memories I have of you—
Are a bright and happy one,
They go all the way back in time—
To the things we shared and done.
Going down memory lane with you—
To see what you've been through,
But you made a way my love—
I am very proud of you.
Even when all hope was gone—
And you lost your guiding light,
You planned by the day my love—
And you dreamed through the night.
You dreamed for God to make a way—
For a new and better life,
From a lonely life of living sorrow—
And hurting bitter strife.
But through your life's struggles my love—
It was hard for you to find,
The meaning of true living and love—
Having a restful peace of mind.
My thoughts have placed me in the past—
To all things we used to do,
As I sit here inside this Prison cell
My memory is only you.

By Terry Webb

"I MISS HER"

Pain in my heart, and my old thoughts abide,
Time hasn't brought relief, somebody lied.
Who told me time, would ease all my pain?
I still miss her, in the weeping of the rain.
I want her back, right beside my side,
If I said otherwise, I would have lied.
Letting her go, I must have been insane,
But inside my heart, my love for her remains!

By Terry Webb

"THINKING OF YOU"

Thinking of you, in all things we used to do,
Dreaming of the things that we've been through.
The magic of our love, still deep within my mind,
Even till this day, I'm still looking to find.
The moment and the time of sweet surprise,
Holding you close to me, looking into your eyes.
I want you to know, that I'm still in love with you,
No matter of your past, no matter what you do.
As long as we live, we belong to each other,
We should try more, to understand one another.
I think of these things my love, all the given time,
I love you more than everything; I hope that's no crime.
You mean so much to me my love; I wish you could see,
How just the very thought of you effect the heart in me.
My mind is always on you, I think of you day and night,
Your love is truly wonderful; you're simply out of sight.
We're holding and we're kissing, sharing deep emotions,
I'm only thinking of you my love, with no other notions.
No matter of your past, no matter what you do.
My mind and heart is always, thinking only of you!

By Terry Webb

"LOVE LIKE OURS"

Thinking of you my love, in all things I do,
Thoughts in my mind are always on you.
A life of love, it is so wonderful to me,
And that's the way, God intended it to be.
Love and affection, within in our heart,
Will care and comfort us, while we're apart.
A love like ours, will never fall,
Like trees on a mountain, keep standing tall.
A love like ours, is hard to find,
A love ours, is one of a kind.
A love like ours, is pure delight,
I long for you, each day and night.

By Terry Webb

"YOU MEAN SO MUCH TO ME"

You mean so much to me; I wish that you can see,
You are my only love, a true love you are to me.
My life is very important, when we're hand in hand,
Now that we are apart, my heart is in demand.
Sometimes I close my eyes, and I see your pretty face,
Suddenly you are here with me, in this lonely place.
I still see the beauty, all the beauty within you,
As I see the morning sunshine, on a sky so blue.
But in my prison cell, I am lonely with a tear,
I am so very far from you, and I miss you my dear.

By Terry Webb

"HOLDING YOU"

Inside my arms, I'll hold you tight,
Until the morn, bring forth its light.
When the light, appear in the skies,
I'll still be looking, in your sweet eyes.

If ever we, should break apart,
And lose the love, inside our heart.
I'll kiss your lips, with a sweet soft kiss,
To remind you of, the love you'll miss.

By Terry Webb

"MY DREAM IS YOU"

My heart is empty, and all alone,
And afraid to except, anyone as my own.
I need someone perfect, and understanding too,
Fun and exciting, in all things she do.
Honest and devoted, to only me,
That's the way our love will have to be.
Maybe I'm expecting, a very whole lot,
But she must give, all the love she got.
This may be, although it may seem,
An unreal fantasy, but it's my dream.
And someday my dream, it will come true,
And in my dream, my dream is you!

By Terry Webb

"THE LOVE WE SHARE"

Nothing means as much to me—
As this special love we share,
A beautiful romantic love affair—
Both of us really care.
A love that only God made true—
This love we share today,
The love between the two of us—
We share in a special way.
Giving all our heart inside—
Together we are true,
Nothing means as much to me—
As the love I share with you.

By Terry Webb

"TRUE LOVE"

To have a love, amazingly true,
Be careful in, the things you do.
To have a love, that's pure and bright,
You have to do, what makes it right.
To have a love, that fills the air,
You must apply God's loving care.
To have a love, forever true,
Give your all, your mate will too.
To make your love, to always last,
You have to blot, away the past.
Then let God live within your heart,
And your love will never, ever part.

By Terry Webb

"YOU'RE MY LOVE"

You are my love, you're my everything,
My heart skips a beat, but joyfully sings.
I call out your name, within my heart,
To give me joy and comfort while we're apart.
As I look towards the heavens, unto the skies,
I see your pretty smile; I see your pretty eyes.
Such a beautiful smile on your pretty face,
I then hold your body, in tight embrace.
But loneliness inside me, in my heart remain,
In reality you're not with me, my heart is still in pain
But you will always be my love and on one special day,
We will be together again, this is what I pray.

By Terry Webb

"A LOVE'S DEFINITION"

This love's definition, defined from me to you,
Explains the facts of love, all things
that we've been through.
In as much a love, that's perfect with a bond,
Greater than the mountains, and oceans beyond.
This is my definition, of a sweet and true love,
Dedicated to you, my tender loving dove.

L- is for the <u>Laughter</u> that we share with each other.
The joy and fun under the sun, we share with one another.

O- is for the <u>Only,</u> the only love that's true,
A love shared by no one else, only me and you.

V- is for the Victory, of love we have won,
Through life's ups and downs, since
the day we had begun.

E- is for the <u>Experience</u>, of all things we've been through.
A life of true devotion, with me loving you.

This loving definition, explains true devotion,
With life and our love, fulfilling all emotion.
Love expresses the value of life, between you and me,
Our love stretches further, than the wide and open sea.
Love is just a four letter word that means a very whole lot,
It means two people devote themselves,
giving it all they got!

By Terry Webb

"WITH YOU ALWAYS"

Forever and always, forever near,
Forever my love is with you dear.
No one or nothing, can take it away,
This love we share, in our special way.

This love we have, will never ever part,
The love we share, deep within our heart.
Until the end time, ending all our days,
My love will be with you, forever always.

By Terry Webb

"MY LOVING GIRL"

My precious, tender, loving dove,
I am lost, without your love.
You mean everything in life to me,
I pray that our love will always be.
I miss that precious little touch,
Of your lips, I love so much.
That sweet warm and gentle kiss,
Is truly what, I really miss.
I will always love you girl,
You're my love, you are my world.

By Terry Webb

"I LOVE YOU"

You are the diamond of my eye
My gem and my pearl
I love you more than everything
In this entire world

I love the beauty of your eyes
And smile upon your face
I love the way you love me girl
I love when we embrace

I love you because you're wonderful
I love you because you're true
But mostly why I love you girl
Is just because you're you.

Terry Webb

ABOUT THE AUTHOR

Terry Webb was born in Birmingham, Alabama on January 12, 1958 to Perry and Cora Mae Webb. In 1976 Terry graduated from High School then enlisted in the army to continue his education. Later he was Honorably Medically Discharged early from the Military due to a service related incident. Life was not the same for Terry after that. Although he found employment, it didn't pay him enough to support his family, so Terry sold drugs on the side to supplement his income. The money was good for awhile until one day Terry was arrested and sent to Prison. He lost everything, including his wife and son. Once he was paroled, Terry tried desperately to put his life back together, but things for him were never the same. The streets of "Watts" Los Angeles became his hustle grounds and also his death trap because the drugs that he sold, he eventually became addicted to them himself. While in his addiction, Terry participated in a program called "Project Build" sponsored by MAXINE WATERS in the Imperial Courts Projects. Terry completed the program and enrolled in South West College but failed due to his drug addiction. After 15 years of struggling in his addiction, going back and forth to Prison, sleeping in vacant houses, abandoned cars and on the side of freeways, digging out of trash cans for scraps, at his lowest point in life, Terry turned his life over to the care of God and asked the Lord Jesus into his heart. God has been in the midst of his deepest struggles and in years time, has now restored everything in Terry's life that was lost in his addiction including his beloved family. This series of events was the birth of Poetry to God, And the inspiration came from God! While serving prison time in California State Prison's, The experience was life changing and has made him a better person and ultimately, he hopes, a better father, husband, man of God and artist. While Terry was imprisoned, he has written more than 1,000 poems and songs. God directed Terry's path through Victory Outreach Ministries, Drug Court, The Royal Palms and Shields For Families to get his life back on track, Terry then became an active member of the "CITY OF REFUGE" and "New Mt CALVARY BAPTIST CHURCH." Now Terry doesn't do anything against the law but works with the law as a Loss Prevention Security Officer. Terry is also a Licensed Ordained Minister and has a Degree in Psychology and Chemical Dependency Counseling. Terry has become a professional helper and demonstrates his impulse to care by going over and beyond the expectations of his role helping others. By the grace of God, his inspirational poems are to help others who are lost so that they may be found in Christ. Terry believes that "POETRY TO GOD" will change the lives of everyone who reads it, one person at a time, and will make the world a better place for everyone to live, one day at a time...

Look for all four Volumes Of
"POETRY TO GOD" online at:

Poetrytogod.org
Trafford.com
Amazon.com
Barnes&noble.com

Poetry to God
Volume 1
Lord Please Hear the Cry

Poetry to God
Volume 2
No Fault Found

Poetry to God
Volume 3
Into Thine Hands

Poetry to God
Volume 4
**Prison Praise,
Cry's From Behind The Wall**

Gas $50.45   B. $41.00
Conf.# T28905